AF322692

This book belongs to:

____

Copyright © 2024 Julia Berdichevskaya

All rights reserved. This book or parts thereof may not be reproduced in any form, stored in any retrieval system, or transmitted in any form by any means—electronic, mechanical, photocopy, recording, or otherwise—without prior written permission of the publisher/author.

WRITTEN BY JULIA BERDICHEVSKAYA   ILLUSTRATED BY NATALIIA MATIUSHKO

THE HAPPY FOOD ADVENTURE

Once upon a time, in a colorful world,
there lived two best friends named
TONY and SONYA.

They loved playing outside and having fun, but they also knew the importance of eating healthy food to grow STRONG and HAPPY.

One sunny day, Tony and Sonya decided to go on a special adventure to learn about healthy eating habits.

They skipped along a path and found a magical garden full of delicious fruits and vegetables. They were amazed by the VIBRANT COLORS and YUMMY SMELLS.

The first stop on their adventure was a big, red apple tree. Tony and Sonya learned that apples are packed with vitamins and fiber that help keep them HEALTHY and STRONG.

They took a juicy bite and felt REFRESHED and ENERGIZED.

Next, they discovered a field of GREEN LEAFY vegetables.

They learned that these greens, like spinach and lettuce, are superheroes that make their bodies GROW TALLER and their eyes SHINE BRIGHTER. Tony and Sonya decided to try a tasty salad with lots of veggies and found it surprisingly delicious.

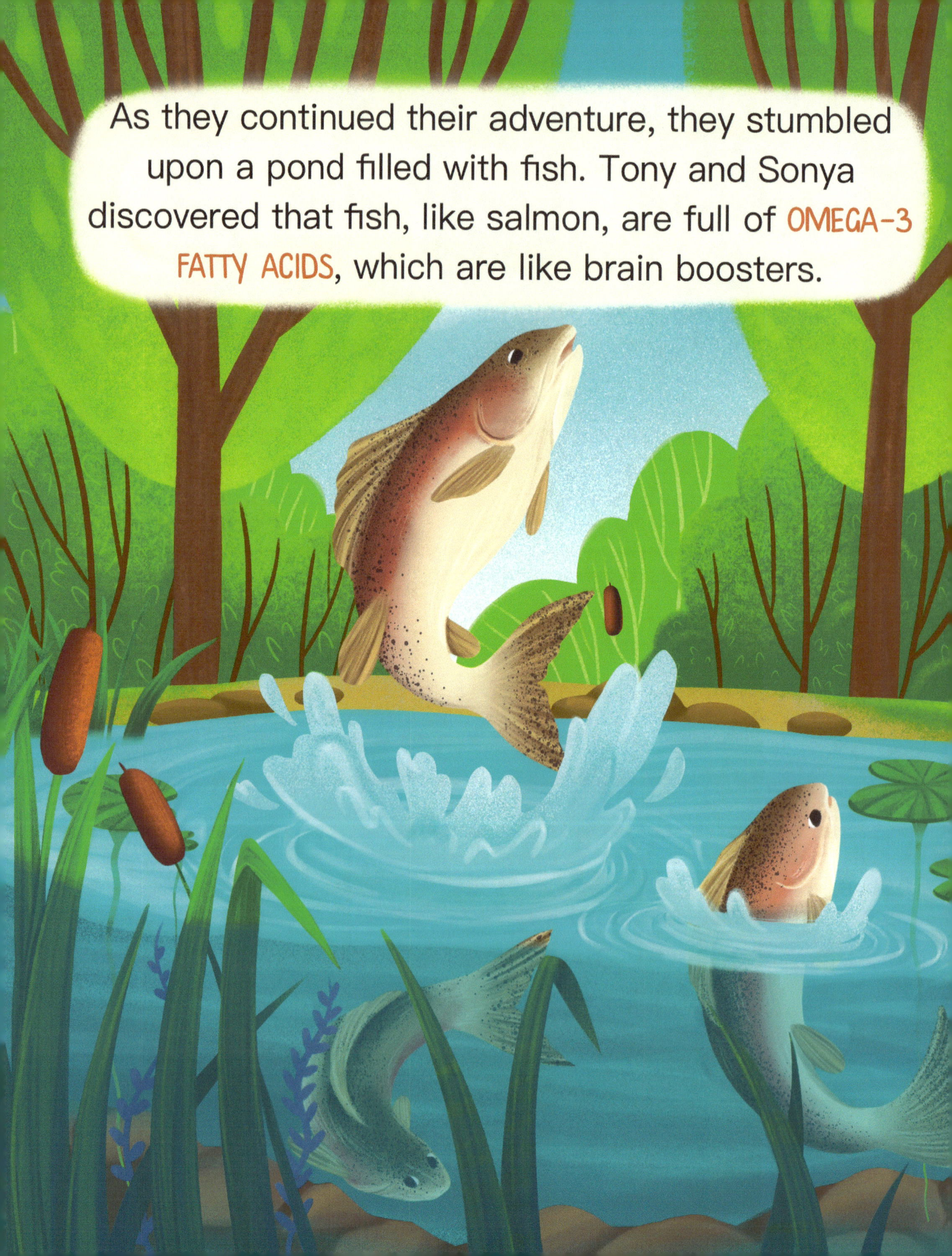
As they continued their adventure, they stumbled upon a pond filled with fish. Tony and Sonya discovered that fish, like salmon, are full of OMEGA-3 FATTY ACIDS, which are like brain boosters.

They giggled and splashed in the water, imagining their brains getting SMARTER and STRONGER.

Finally, they found a beehive buzzing with activity. The bees taught them about the sweet treasure they make – honey. Tony and Sonya learned that honey is a NATURAL SWEETENER that is better for their bodies than sugary treats. They dipped their fingers into a jar of honey and savored the natural sweetness.

With their bellies full and their minds brimming with newfound knowledge, Tony and Sonya returned home, ready to share their healthy eating adventure with their friends and family. They realized that eating fruits, vegetables, fish, and honey was not only good for them but also made them FEEL HAPPY INSIDE.

From that day forward, Tony and Sonya made sure to eat a rainbow of colorful fruits and vegetables every day. They grew up STRONG, SMART, and FULL OF ENERGY, and their friends joined them on their happy food adventure too.

Remember, my little friends, eating HEALTHY food is like a MAGICAL journey for your body. So, hop on board and embark on your very own happy food adventure!

THE HAPPY FOOD
ADVENTURE
COLORING PAGES

HONEY

HONEY

www.ingramcontent.com/pod-product-compliance
Lightning Source LLC
Chambersburg PA
CBHW042322140726
48196CB00015B/698